Suicide Stop It Now!
Help Is On The Way!

1). Look Up!

2). Post-Traumatic Stress Disorder.

3). Getting Through It.

4). There Is A Reason For Everything!

5). Respect And Understand Why

You Should Be Respected!

6). Non-Sleep Awards.

2

7). Are You Thinking About Yourself Again?

8). Support Of A Better Way Of Living!

9). Something That Is Most Important!

Look Up!

My name is Johnnie H Williams Jr. I am writing this book on suicide stop it now, and PTSD got to keep it moving! A lot of things have happened in my life, and not only to assist veterans but many other people. The fact of the matter is that this is something, that is affecting people of all walks of life. When you walking down the street, out to dinner late at night with a friend; somewhere along the line you will end up hearing. The good the bad the ugly things of life, which always find a way back into our lives. Why is it that the good, never outweigh the bad: as much as the ugly? The heaviness of the heart which beats the joys of the happiness of life. Which upon working them both together, one can produce the spoils of this great life. How many classes can one take, in order to educate one's life? How many educations one take, in order to know the number of classes one should take in life. From day one till this day I am still taking classes, to educate my life. Into the future of living a better way of life; be careful what you ask for. When you start out to be yellow, brown, black, blue, green, purple, red, white, gray. This is true for this we have seen, is the future, colors of the hairstyles of the future! Are you thinking of your future at this moment, you'll be surprised where your future ends up; but it time you get there? I'm writing this book on suicide because I have been there before. For all of you who read this book, I hope that you understand it. The time spent for me to put it together, is the knowledge put from my brains and years of suffering with pain and agony. I am not the only other person who has went into these types of things, I have talked to many about this in the past; I'm not sure how much time I have left. Because of many factors that I am being put in place, it may not be too long before I might be on the other side of that ridge. Either way it makes no difference to me, from that point of view I will still kick your butt; get you out of that house and keep you on the move. Veterans go through hell as well as many of the human beings do also. Just like 90.3 FM radio in which every first Monday of the month. This is a all veterans radio talk show. We host our talk show! Many times, we talk about the 22 veterans, per day that commit suicide, in case you haven't heard the number has gone up. Have you ever thought the reason why veterans are doing this? Have you ever thought of the reason why veterans doing this I will ask you once again? I can only get in trouble for the words which I speak to come out of my mouth, therefore. Let's be honest about all we must talk about. When a man cries is from his heart being broken. Once a woman cries is from her heart being broken. Do we understand each other. When a human being cries is from their hearts and souls being broken. Some veterans wherever they may be especially on our front line, when they come home; everyone who sees them hearts are broken. Suicide you have no idea what it's about, nor do you doctors not do this psychiatrist. But there's a blessing that offered those who do listen and take the time to understand us. They call it post-traumatic stress disorder today, should I say what they called it before today who would it matter to. It would matter to those who were at that time needed help! Suicide what kind of crazy world can that be, there is no such thing as a crazy world known as suicide. How do I know, you really want to know how do I know? Anyone who has ever asked for help, has been given a blessing in life. It is not how many times you have received that blessed. It is if you follow through, with each blessing; one day at a time. I pray all day; I prayed all night; for a better life. I know of the words here today gone tomorrow! It is what I can do while I am here, to show you that he is always near; that's why it is nothing for you to fear. I know that there will be many who read what I have to say, I hope you understand in so many ways. Understand that what I say, has already been throughout the land; this is just for those who need that special helping hand. Suicide prevention there is a way, for a long time I've been saying the words help is on the way! I came home from Vietnam had nowhere to go, I walked amongst my family. But my friends are in Vietnam still alone. I cried every day and every night. Because I had left them there, and for some reason that I did not know; Uncle Sam had dropped my ass right here. I set up on the roof tops, late at night looking at the moonlight; wishing I was back in Vietnam in the fight. The nightmares came, every night and I did not know what to do. I went through so much hell, for so many years. I lived in my mother's house, for less than a year. I had to leave my mother's house, because I started carrying weapons. I moved into my own apartment, got a job and went to college. Never wanted to stay home alone. When I stayed home alone was the biggest problems, because when I went to sleep. the nightmares started; the screaming started; the yelling started. The police started knocking at the door, one of the things I had to start doing was give up drinking. I can't believe I just said that, you can't believe it either if you are alcoholic; or addicted to everything in life. The neighbors call because you are screaming like a crazy person, everyone scared as hell of you and they better be, you do think yourself as a person who's always ready. Could you imagine the crazy things that Vietnam vets do, I would climb up the side of a six-story building to get into my house. I locked myself out of the house, keys on the table. I enjoy jumping from one roof to the other roof, no matter what floor it was; hoping i would miss the roof? This way all can come to an end and all would be over with a flash; that would be the end of the show. can you see my crazy way of thinking, this was my easy way out and this is only one of many ways of doing it? There was a movie back in the day, which a man played a role where they play Russian roulette. But all my drinking and all my thinking I still remember the three times that I tried it. Therefore, I can say between the roof jumping and the three different occasions it was the dumbest things that a person can do. And you really think that that's the only thing that I tried to do to end it not even close. A person gets so frustrated in their life and just say enough is enough because they believed that the time is come and can just walk away from it; this is not true. I was blown across the dam bunker, fine okay it wasn't time. Crash in a new car 145 miles an hour, motor in the front seat; trunk in the front seat. Car spending upside down, a new car the next day. MAD as hell is not even never mind come out of my mouth. Anger you have no idea, what it is for a human being to be as angry as one human being can be. To look at you and not act in 1/10 of a second, this totally impossible for me not to do. A scorpion with a sting, is the only thing I know how to do. suicide anyone who enters the end zone, and you recognize this. Action must be taken, at once.

Before you can even think of, recovery zone! we haven't even talked about post-traumatic stress disorder yet. Of course, I am not an expert on any, distinguished category you might want to call it. Except for I'm alive for the next 10 seconds therefore while I'm here allow me to talk. The problem is there are so many people willing to hear what you get to say. Out of 100, 90 really understand what you're talking about. PTSD as it is also called, is in many forms and shapes and sizes. They also caused by trig, in my case helicopters fireworks and all the above. Also had to control myself when other people, feel that they are more pushy shell I say then I am. In other words when a human being becomes disrespectful, that's a no-no. I respect everyone in every way shape or form. We fought for our country America, do not disrespect us. Means do not. PTSD, or post-traumatic stress disorder; is a life of hell that we all had to go through. When I came home from Vietnam, I was dropped off. Stay locked in my room for three days. No one said anything except for how you are and know we'll talk. Because they didn't know what to say, understand what I'm saying. 25 years later, I found help. I am not the first one and I will not be the last so, if your wife or your husband. You think is acting strange or has a problem, yes, they do and no it is not because of you. Also, if you think you can change them for the better, you are wrong; they need some help. This is the reason why I'm writing this book, because suicide is no joke, and you think that is over and I'm doing just fine. Why in the hell do you think I'm writing this book right now. Suicide and my 4 strokes 3 heart attacks, stomach cut open stomach swollen up like a 6-month pregnant woman. After 47 years in the gym, doctors gave permission to go back to the gym. One year out of the gym, 30 days ago could have been back in the gym; back in six days. I love the gym and all it does for me. My PTSD has been on the rise, I have seen my suicide on the horizon; slowly showing me the way back. We must be the ones to talk about these things, they just do not go away; help is on the way are the words I use. One of the words that you use in your life I pray every day; I pray every night. You have no idea what the hell goes on in life, when others are going through hell; do you really think they care. You must be the one to stand up, I saw myself standing tall and did not pay attention to what I was supposed to be doing. Of course, I paid for it and it did happen to me. Doing all the things for our veterans and families that I am supposed to do; with all the support and when I turned around and then I looked up that's when I got the message. Not everything that you think is going to be there, will be there. When your love comes from your heart, and your strength come from within and you are able to move those mountains without the fear which comes up with in that's when you say the words thank you father for this day and everything in it.

You must remember that from within your heart, is where it starts if your dream is real; it must be made of steel. Only God's love, can come from above which is called help is on the way! You got to remember that out there is help that can be found, it is so amazing that all the hell that I haven't gone to my whole life. I have been able to find help. There is a difference in finding the different types of help that one needs. In our James J peters Medical Center, Dr. Julia Golior she is a life saver. Dr. Julia Golior is a true-life saver she saved my life. It's hard for me to explain to you I know does the system that set up that many will talk to you, but if you understand it is not like one can see yeah, I understand you. It's not like that! For years we have worked together in so many ways, through the James J peters VA system I have turned into a better person. Finding my family of veterans where we managed to come closer to each other talking with each other and caring for each other. I can remember the days of my PTSD was thousand times worse than what it is at this moment. I can say to you, if I could have landed there early in life: you could've had a better life this could not be true. The moments that we all have and see, a moment of happiness and sadness. As we age and time we try to move forward in life at a better attitude and think of those soon to come behind us. I'm living to make a better life for all of us, not for some of us. I always have my wife ANA and Christina my baby girl in mind 24 hours a day. Our company help is on the way 1020 CORP, will be a wonderful company one day that will help all Veterans families move forward in life. In Vietnam I was attach to the 199 light infantry 4/12 (TET1968). Vietnam was nothing that I would like to talk about. But for the sake of all of veterans who came home. I would like to say welcome home; we are all family and we are here for you. You must take the time out to find help, you cannot live by yourself and go through life like this. If you are reading this book, it is about suicide and about PTSD is post-traumatic stress disorder, our up and down in life. Ask for help now! There are so many things that we need to talk about, the nights and not sleeping all of the thoughts that is on the mind. The problems of not paying the rent/electric bills/telephone bills/water bills/all the above. Sometimes we need to talk to someone, but there's really no one to talk to. There is still the same old johnnieh@mindspring.com send email / website

helpisonthewayforveterans.net and just say Johnnie I
like to speak. Those nightmares are real, can you
imagine how many times a helicopter flies over head,
what I go through. For me all set of whose helicopter.
Channel 5/7/12/ channel 2 or even the national guard's
chopper. They all triggers for me and for you. I am only
speaking on some of the things that I go through and I
have not even touch on a third of them. Yes, I have a
nice smile, just like everyone else. But remember the
title war is hell, is one of the reasons I don't sleep most
of the year. Most of the time I sleep, I'm back in
Vietnam; I need not tell people where what I've done
nor been.

Suicide on the problem of all veterans, of every war 22 a
day was the number. Hello suicide prevention Everyone
thinks is just one error of veterans not true, what is
needed is to save every veteran. It is the thoughts that
is in our minds, that is putting us in the positions that
we are in. When we need help who was there, to hear
the words that we are saying! Not only who's hearing
the worst that we say, who only trusting that
understanding these words we are saying. Is it possible
to say of how many times, a person must sit in front of
someone; before they break down can really start. How
many times must someone enter in, before the agony of
defeat; jumps right. How many times must one tell the
story, where they get to that same point in time where
they did not want to go. How many times did you make

me go to, when I asked you not to do it; when you knew I didn't want to go. Some of us came home, many of us did not; my brothers and sisters I miss you.
I understand and I see you and I feel you and I love you. I cry for you and I tried to die for you and now I try to live for you. We must show all those, who are here this day; why we say the words help is on the way! Of all our pain and our suffering, of all the ups and downs of life; those words God bless America that we have fought for. Are why our veterans, has got to stand tall in life.

Yes, I am 70 years young, and I am back in the gym. You might think I'm a little slow, but yes, I don't think so. If I am called, I will show up, as a Vietnam veteran; my job is 24 hours a day. In the USA. As I walked this land in the day or the night, I'm here for any kind of fight. To protect this land, and my family first; this many who you see. Who believe in liberty, not only will we protect our land; will make sure America stays free? Make no mistake about it, of what I mean by standing tall. God bless America! Is God bless America for all. Respect all veterans with a better understanding, past this word throughout the land; to put a stop to this suicide as it stands! This post-traumatic stress disorder can you not see. Do you not understand, why the hell is happening to me? Yes, you're right? I'm 70 years old. 70 years young? Maybe I'm not sure which one?

Sounds like PTSD to me. Or someone is trying to
question your way of thinking? Psychologically thinking
one word for me to you, why would it take 69 years to
diagnose me with posts traumatic stress disorder? One
must understand this; many have called me a human
computer. My way of thinking I believe they're right,
and I believe they're wrong. I believe the right because
there are not too many questions that I can't answer, in
helping people find a better way of life. I believe there
wrong because I don't think, computers can cry like a
baby when I feel the pains of life. I'm being honest with
you because I want everyone to stop hurting
themselves. Find a better way of life. I want your wives
to help the husband's and the husband to help the
wives. Sons and daughters to help the fathers and the
mothers. The simple fact is if we don't help each other
as a family, that family is going to fall apart. Did you
know that I have, fell out of a helicopter with my 60-
machine gun? In the wrong LZ and was hanging down
when they pulled me back in. I was stuck halfway in the
mud and they were yelling wrong LZ wrong LZ. I can't
believe that, had been on my mind from speaking to
you at this moment. But you should believe that
daytime turned into nighttime over there, or even that a
phantom fighter; you can almost touch it with your
hand. Talking about having nightmares, these are not
about my nightmares. They about the nightmares, of

you yourself. Those words haunt me every time I turn around again, war is hell. I refrain from telling you, What I would want to tell you! I have tried my best, to get help throughout the years. You cannot go to the hell that we have, all these many years. It makes no sense, for any human to have to live this way. For us so many victims' families, live a life of hell from post to traumatic stress disorder. Families talk to me day and night; I've been doing this before 1990. You can't take this job from me if you tried, this life he has given unto me. I remember more than 27 years ago, the lady called me up: no food in the house for me and my daughter. 3 o'clock in the morning, open my refrigerator door put a lot of food in the shopping bags. I went to this lady's house, knocked on the door; lady opened the door say what the hell. I set food down and said I'll see you later, she said I can't believe you bought this here Johnnie; I said God bless America and I went home. I've had many / nights of nightmares and one of the best ways for me to turn my life around was to work at night. What I also found out was that I had to go to school, there was something about education that was in my brain that would not stop. This thing about suicide I just could not stop it. Somewhere in the horizon was this suicide. I will be going to bars and I was drinking, and I was smoking marijuana and I was getting into fights. I was always a gentleman; I was very respectful to all and when the time came; not those who thought they can whip my butt.   It didn't happen that easy and they found out the hard way. That the scorpion does have a sting. I found myself working going to college and at the college going to work and then going to sleep. This is hard to do, but I did it in order not to sleep. This book is not just about me, I keep saying that to you; you must understand. Life is hell when you don't find help. Lots of veterans, which we're talking about; and our families which we can add in. Now/or the future. Because this will happen, sooner or later. Do you want me to tell you of how many times, I had taken my 60-machine gun and went bananas? Or should I take a worst moment that I had, that freaked me out, I just looked at the person stands in front of me. Then I walked away. Sometimes you got to understand, others don't know the power you have; you don't have to show it to them. Just because you have it, does that mean; everyone must know that you have it. Whenever you in the VA hospital in the Bronx, you be so surprising the love we share. secret agents are good people, who love to put a smile on your face. Did you know that by sharing our love, will make someone's day better? Would you believe it that my butt was blown across, the other side of a bunker along with three other guys. Would you believe we all got up and dust ourselves off and laughed and the Sgt. called us idiots? We were young and dumb we went down.   Things that happen to you, as a veteran it was your job to do; it wasn't until later. When you lay down to sleep, that the dam nightmares began to creep; it's night that you hit the field. Everyday tears in your eyes would appear, of the fears that did appear of other veterans' lives and friends. These nightmares kept coming one after the other, causing you to start to drink day in and day out. Not knowing the reason why, they were coming, he was sent back out into the field. You are living in pure hell, not knowing if you were going in; but you will be coming out. Only thing I cared about was, 800 bullets a minute; and to lock and load. The anger part showed up, whenever we lost someone; wasn't really a reason why we lost that person. Did we do the right thing while we were out there. Could we possibly find a person to blame for this, can we find and you're so interested that they are so yes I guess those are some good reading their yeah and the helicopter part they are not all the stuff and in our sin crazy stuff yes on this on this up with this good stuff and this held a standing start messing me up this damn computer is. Check for me here yet is also turned out to change the wording and there to kick for this. I was told there is a reason for everything. Post-traumatic stress disorder is exactly what you have, this is what is called at this time; understand this before it changes now. Grab that computer step forward and educate thyself now. You serve your country, thank you for your service; take care of you and your family now! Veterans come to get the now as one, as on the battlefield leave no one behind.

We must care for each other and this must be done now! Remember I told you about Dr. Julia Golior. One of the reasons I spoke to you about Dr. Julia Golior. Is because, I have had many doctors before I spoke with her. As time went on and we started talking and understanding each other. A trust factor came into a greater value, at which point I needed to be locked down. I just got married I just had a newborn baby girl, and I had just got locked down. And my doctor said this is the best time for me to have this done. You may not believe this, but Dr. Julia Golior is my guardian angel. Dr. Julia Golior you cannot take that job from her if you try to, she is a blessing to all veterans. And they will fight if you try to take her away from them. I was locked down at the right time and the only problem was, I was one of 33% of veterans who you can't all lock down overnight. So, after the third day they took me out and gave me a card the punch and every Monday at 8 o'clock and punch out 3 o'clock every afternoon. Vietnam is one reason why it can't be locked down at night. Nightmares a real suicide is a real Russian roulette 3 times was real. You understand that is you that you try to save, the person who's going through this problem in their life. Whichever person is going through things in their life, how would you like me to say this; to the person who's going to the problem in this life. Are you the one who was going through the problem, in this life? Understanding the things that I'm saying to the person, who was going through the problems in this life. Comprehension of the problem, of the person going through the changes in this life. Help is on the way! If you are reading, or if someone is reading to you; understand this. In my books help is on the way/ help is on the way2/ the mustard seeds/ when change comes go to bed will you be ready. I've been to hell 10 times, and the devil was absent; it 10 times he and my books. The devil knew I was, and each time, even he got the hell out of there. Have faith in our father in heaven, he is always near; even when you may think he's not he is there. You may not believe in a lot of things, that's okay and I understand why; I have seen so many things of the future still to come. I have always been 3 to 4 years ahead of time and just about everyone knows this; educate yourself and move forward in life. With the help of our VA hospitals, our vet centers and many others willing to help all who have served to our country. We will all find a better way to move forward in life, working for a better life to care for all families. Suicide prevention can be acted upon by many people, who may see people along the way in need of help. Sometimes by listening to what people had to say, we may find out that this person may be asking for help; they don't even know that this is what they are asking for. They are also signs of post-traumatic stress disorder all these different signs; would you believe you can go cool and as we find out for yourself. I am a recovering alcoholic 30 years recovering drug addict marijuana 30 years cigarette smoker 30 years one day at a time. There is nothing you cannot do one day at a time. I was in the gym for 47 years. That's given night I got sick and went to the VA hospital. Couple of days later, they pulled the black warm out of my stomach. Next thing you know I was several months pregnant. I was told not to go back to the gym for one year, what is it died then; may not be in the gym. One year was up like an alcoholic was afraid to take a drink. I was scared to go back in the gym. Three months later, I walked back in the gym; and I started working out again. I felt like a superstar and went overboard and did a pull down at 100 pounds. Had to slow down and get my head back together. I'm ready for my workout now, full speed ahead! For you for reading this book yes, they are still nightmares, and don't you forget this but is to hope that you stop and get help. That will take away most of the pain. Be honest with thyself, for what it is that you want to do best with thyself; is the only way to enter in. Do you think they can take those dreams out of your head, which one of us do you think; they going to fool. This year is the 50th anniversary for me of the Vietnam veteran. Did you just get the message! Psychiatry is at its best working together. Only when that trust factor enters in, when I am going through my hell; my honesty must be @ its best. The in cognitive of my self-explanatory insufficient is inconsistent of how I am feeling now in time. If you have ever seen me break down, it is only because the trust or the love i have for you. If you have ever seen me go off, you in the wrong place at the wrong time. I'm still thinking of when I stuck the gun down the man's throat, in the hallway of my mother's apartment building. When my mother came out the apartment, said put that gun away and let that man go. Whatever you do don't bring the gun back in my house, and I said oh mom really! I lived in my mom's house another month. I moved into my own apartment, like mom said I had to give up the gun. Life change not for the better for the worse, but I ended up getting more guns, then Russian roulette came to play. The drinking and the thinking and the smoking and the choking those are the days suicide was crazy as hell I'm telling you these things, so you don't get in that dark, tunnel I was in. I am hoping none of you will ever be in a dark tunnel, that I was in it is hard to come out. you can't do things by yourself family sometimes it's hard to ask for help I'm telling you about suicide and I'm telling you about post-traumatic stress disorder. One of the hardest things in life and I'm the one telling you is to be honest with your own self, when you find out things about your own self it is hell. What you will find out the next day in life, are things you really thought you know about. Sometimes your way of thinking, is way beyond reach. Why is it that we sometimes think things like this, it's a way of thinking in this point of time? How many of us are screamed all night, how many has screamed some of the night? How many have not screamed at all. Can you contemplate what I just said, yes and no of the answers. You may read between the lines, but only if you have an open mind. Being capable does not mean that you are reliable, nor does being reliable means that you are capable. Suicide stop it now, is the path that I'm putting you on; by the words to which I choose for you to understand. For with you now read all the real deeds, in which you the reader will have to achieve. To not only live in hell, wander all day and night in hell; try to figure out how the hell to get out of hell. Look up he will help you on your way. Only if you believe in yourself and not in what others want you to believe; by standing tall you also come out of it all. Suicide stop it now. If you really think that I am the only one, who has felt deep in this cave; on my knees I pray to get out of here in any way. Suicide many think of can be such a joke, is worse than any heart attack or a stroke. The four times I did try, what the hell makes you think I'm still alive. With AA/NA/VA. All the crybaby tears do for, of every event that shows up; I forget how to grow up. Now I lay me down to sleep, why in the hell that had to say the words sleep; here comes the tears and fears along with all those creeps. Without the power of my veteran's love, I would not be here; to share my family love.

It's when you see your son/daughter/father/mother's love. Understand that veterans have been in hell, loves you more than they can tell. We cannot tell you the things that we've been through, but you will never be able to sleep either boo! I Love you for being here and love you for being near and I enjoy happiness throughout the years. When you see the signs, then I'm acting strange and alone; help me to see some counseling. This way I won't end up living in life all alone, most effectively I have learned from my past; not to stand up and start yelling like an ass. When you guessed it at point when I'm not behaving myself, my only love That time I need some help. Never sit there say those words that he will be okay, those are only the words that will never make my day. Nightmares on bad feelings they will never go away, how can I notice for 50 years and is still with me today. Help is on the way is my model! I love these words I say, hoping that many others will find with a blessing; the words come true each day. there comes a time when you see me do things, that you may have thought could not have been me. We all have all triggers and me was cabdrivers. I remember my love the day was Mother's Day. Of course, the cab driver kept driving fatly behind me. Also, he decided to blow his horn a couple of times, and then when the light turned green, he decided to blow his on one more time. As I got out Ana's car and he got out of his, I think I move faster than him; he saw my face and said the words. I'm sorry Mr. veteran, I stopped, and it turned off just in time if it weren't for those words. I got back into my car and my wife handed me my rubber armbands. She had grabbed them off me, as I ran out of the car. We are not here to do harm to anyone only to love our family and our country. I am ready 29 hours a day and will always be ready 29 hours a day. Suicide prevention we must stop, all these things by finding help now. I've only told you of some of the things, in which I have done. There is a much larger list of things, in which I could've hurt my own self. Look deep into thy family's eyes, take the time to feel the pains; in which you are responsible for. When I came home a gentleman by the name of Mr. Sampson, informed me that it was not my family fault to what I have been through. This was the first time in my life, that I stop blaming others for the problems that I had It was the first time in my life, that something was so got damn clear. Mr. Sampson taught me a hell of a lot, case in point. I hated the government, he said who was the government. I couldn't answer him, I hated them no longer. We all have problems in life, talk about them and hell no do not cry. How do I feel today, don't even try it. I'm still 18 years old/take my word for it.

Post-Traumatic Stress Disorder.

This is part two of this in my mind, I made it through the suicide in my mind; but on the horizon it still sits. The fact of the matter is post-traumatic stress disorder is at the front door and is not helping at all. With so much going on in your mind, when you stay guard duty 29 hours per day; when you have this thing called all around vision. Able to see to your deep right and left. This thing that is now call posts traumatic stress disorder, or PTSD is something not easy to live with. Understand one thing, look at me in any way shape or form that you may want to. I don't want you to think of anyone other than me. No good feelings no bad feeling there's nobody to talk about. Just don't want to be angry with. Just me. Now outcomes the words, does this guy know what he is talking about; it's got to be some throne what this meant brain. I can't believe they let him out of six b, is this guy for real; what is the smoke and orange juice. The most important thing on this earth, is to stop the 22 people per day from committing suicide; and find a better way to deal with PTSD. I can tell you but some of the people going to live and at home and hell, as they talk with me and I am there to help them. A good friend of mine told me today, Johnnie people say you don't help them, you pick up the phone. My good friend is correct, the only problem is. Is he talking about at the same time while I'm helping somebody on the phone, that they are calling me? Or is it the ones who know what they should do but won't get up off their ass; and get the claims done. All the veterans with smiles on their faces, is because the great work that they do; not the work that I do. Every class veteran that I work with, will tell you I called them secret agents; they go out and do their own work. I am nothing but the stop sign. When you stop at the stop sign, this is when you come to the intersection and this when you go in the right direction to get the job done. This is the reason why we call it. Help is on the way! PTSD is everywhere and when you have a hard time talking to people trying to understand the way of life you try to do. Can you imagine coming out the hell, explaining to people what you did while you were in hell; then going back to sleep that night and gone back to hell. How many people really stop and see it this way, how many psychiatrists/therapists/social workers; do we send home the same way. Do you know the full outcome of people working in the VA system, the vet centers, and of the entity? Post-traumatic stress disorder can wear a person down, to do all the above things that I have mentioned in this book. All the people I have mentioned in this book, don't even have to be veterans in this book. Once again as a human computer, the facts go in and the brains fall out.

Getting Through It.

You may think there's some of the hardest times of your life, are economically problems, which pop up out of nowhere. Not true of the dreams of the future, in which we try to better ourselves; that somehow always seem to fall apart. Many call the ups and downs of life, a more effective way of saying to yourself; how in hell did this happen. The only purpose in life is to move forward, what could possibly go wrong with this though. They are called roadblocks and they are set up everywhere that you don't possibly see. Our thoughts of life are true to the fact, of making America better. What many calls the American dream, of looking on the faces of our family members; and being proud of the work which we have done. No one said that life would be easy, this is because each one teaches one. The words getting through it, of the thoughts of the day; that have gone by. You cannot please everyone, nor can you say I love you to someone thousand times a day. You can reach your hand out to help someone and get slapped right in your face. At your boardroom beating, you can try to make them understand; at the end of the day only one person will shake your hand. Some could give a damn, of what you have to say; just pay the bills and kindly be on your way. Don't you ever forget these words I'm about to say, here today and gone tomorrow got dammit is just another day. Of all of you who are now growing up, and don't have the time to knock on the door; I want you to know that I love you before you come to get me and I go out the door. I understand sometimes we can't say, how much we love each other; in so many ways. But I Johnnie H Williams Jr. Have told you more ways someone, come on out before they turn us over then your ass is done. Getting through it hurts in so many ways, because if you are reading this; I wasn't with you enough each day. Getting through it is about all of you who are call friends, the good the bad and the ugly. The ones who wanted to be worked as one, and the others who only wanted to work to get what they needed; and the others who just don't give a damn. Getting through it is when I reach my hand out to you, when you are going through hard times; you came out with a smile. Getting through it when you are sad and didn't know what to do/I was sad and didn't know what to do, we both ended up smiling. I could talk about the times, of whom we lost and those hard time; but we still all getting through it. You who are my family and I don't have to say who you are. I'm not going to keep telling you how much I love you, for one day will end up in outer space. Many know how far I have traveled before time and time and after time. Life is not a joke, does the youth of today; show them now that you do. I was watching the television and I saw today a man getting a street named after him. He is alive and well, finally they on naming streets with the people who are still alive. I am the type of person who looks at these type of things, moonwalks/time travels/visions of the future to come. Getting through it will only happen, when you learn to think, with that open mind. I had just enough time to say to my mother, how much I love her; but not enough time to go back down to see her. Do you think they will come see me, then knock on my door; we call it the future still to come. God bless America!

There Is A Reason For Everything!

From the time that you open your eyes in the morning, until the time that they close at night. Is there a possibility, or the probability of something you have done right? Out on that journey each day, was there a reason why you went that way; or the probability of how it would end up that day. The prognosis points to the conclusion, of the possibility of how you ended that day. A veteran in compact at that point in time, was pulled the trigger does not think of the time. It is a reason for everything, I was told and drill; to pull the trigger it is a skill. Within my site I don't look to the right, I'll pull the dam trigger and say good night. This is a reason for everything, make sure that is understood; this is how we came home understood. Is a reason for everything, this is understood; is a well-trained veteran I can live in the woods. It is a reason for everything, this should be understood no matter what age I may be, as a veteran I'm good. Diagnose me in any way, program/dialysis/psychiatry/nut job. This is a reason for everything, why I am back in the gym; just to make sure you don't punch me on my chin. It is a reason for everything, when I hit the floor i should do another 20 push-ups; before I go out that door. I understand that not all of us can stand, then I want to know this is how veterans flow. We love and care for each other, in so many ways throughout the years. There is a reason for everything, want the tears coming down my face, when most of the night I think of all our sacrifice. How many of you can say, you understand these words I say? Your brains exploded, was that gun ever loaded; did you use a knife never think about the sacrifice. How many times the people he used scream, how many times the people ask you to leave. How many times have you got down on your knees, how many times have you said father please help me? 1968 Tet Offensive 199 light infantry, till this day the tears will not go away. It is a reason for everything, I'm sorry in case you did not know. Of all the things that we call reasons, God our father is the only one who knows. You don't have to be a veteran, or even the St. just to have your brains fall out and faint. Each day of my life, and no I am not alone, because they are many other people traveling on the same road. Don't you ever forget that our father is near, and that light will appear. There is a reason for everything each time I have walked away. Suicide stop it now. Complex ability of the human brain's capacity and flexibility in accessibility no accountability. This can only happen to you, when you don't find a way to look up and say thank you father for this day and everything in it. There is a reason for everything, when you land in hell; pull out the guns and begin to yell. Every day, my father will show me the way. Is a reason for everything, one of the best things to do is to learn; how to reason. I have been down and out and not the only one down and out I had to be in the foxhole, like others in that foxhole; loving the hell that it was. Do you know or understand the word survivor? Many do also many thinks they do, many believed they do; others feel they do. God bless every one of you, I would not want to be in your boots for any reason at all. The reason I say this, is to be able to come home. When others are not able to come home, and you wish they were able to come home with you. But the worst circumstances beyond your control, that did not allow this to happen. Therefore, we call survivors; in our cases the dreams will not go away. He is a reason for everything/AA/NA/PTSD/war.

Respect And Understand Why

You Should Be Respected!

Every human being should be respected, no matter how old they may be; this is a true understanding. It is in this instance, by this millennium in which we are speaking, about veterans. The comparison can only be the understanding, of entering in and coming out some call being discharge. Upon entering in you can only be a civilian, upon departure you are military, with the discharge of your tour of duty. I myself love respect and do not ask for it, it has already been earned; under the words God bless America. This is one thing no human being, can never take away from this human being, who has served his country. Many as myself are proud and make no mistake of how you walk, and you talk of the country I have served. The word respect this I do understand, and it runs throughout this land. My father my uncle my daughter my son and many others have served. Do not disrespect me, for I have no reason

to disrespect you. I asked you not for your respect,
because you must walk with respect, as one who
already understands respect. I am on guard duty on day
and night, but my PTSD I'm always ready for the fight.
In your mind you think that you have called the way,
just knowing Johnnie H Williams has just come out to
play. I am a soldier in my father's Army.

Respect is loving the enemy not hating them,
understanding the way that they think, opening your
mind to the thoughts. Getting down in the dirt,
swimming under the water when no one can even see
you. Walking around late in the cold night air, while
how I love this fear; hoping no one will be near. Do you
know what it is to lay on the ground, laying there for
hours not making a damn sound; knowing if anyone
moved to it would be the end of that fool. There is no
place I rather be, then to lay here on my; in all this mud
just to prove to the enemy he is wrong on this night.
Have no fear I know he's near, it's a damn shame; that
they don't know I am here! You the reader must
understand this is how us veterans have walked this
land, of course you and I with us and still do
understand. Respect with honor is how we stand. I
haven't said much of those who have not come home.
But we see them in many a place, they are never far this

you may not understand; but you were not with us back
there in the land. When you do hear me scream and
holler sorry for all the noise. I ended up someplace I
recognize but that a choice. We love you family
sometimes it happens to us, and if anyone tells you it
will end. Don't believe it. Today I went to the gym and it
was my six-day back, I'm very happy for this. My
tummy is about seven months big, because of the
operation. I have had 47 years in the gym, 443 days out
of the gym. My six-day back and by the time I got to the
pull down. I think I went a little PTSD and went from 70
pounds to 160 pounds pull down. It was then when I
heard someone, yelling and screaming and it was me.
With tears in my eyes each one 10 times each from 70
pounds up and my PTSD set in. Little did I know the
people watching this veteran, go through his thing. The
gym has been my life, while I am able to do this; four
strokes and three heart attacks belly cut open. Respect
is still looking to kick someone's ass, the American way.
Suicide stop it now. Post-traumatic stress disorder.
There is help there for you, as you see all the things that
I'm going

through and still going through in my life. 70 years
young and I'm not done. No matter what condition you
may be in, get up and start all over again. Respect
thyself by standing tall, then keep through it all. Can
you possibly imagine me being a stop sign, it is the best
job in the world? When you go to the library to read a

cookbook, what would happen if the book could talk back to you. But with the understanding of you knowing how to cook, but it only showed you a better way to. It is the work in which my father has given me, 29 hours a day 7 1/2 days a week 875 days a year. Yes, I know try to figure that out and by the way they are few of us who can. Respect each other by standing tall and honoring the words God bless America!

Non-Sleep Awards.

This is a very touchy subject, your calculations of 2+2 = 4; where off many others heard 2×22 equal 44. This is a concept of not paying attention, that happens many a times when you the reader; do not pay attention to the words being said. Stop suicide now, there are many reasons why this can be done. Non-sleep awards are for, all who cannot sleep; not for those who don't want to sleep. Understood! I did not say anything about your doctor, know your medicine in which you are now taking. Sunday morning April 4, another award. I want to do best security guards in the world, why would I say this simply because. I can hear the 747 flying by, late at night or the police helicopter circling the area news

chopper. Our neighbors dog barking, each time
somebody walks past their house. You can hear
husband and the wife, who sometimes end up in a fight
I hope and pray that it won't last all night. Then that cat
in the back, or someone is scratching her back. A lot on
your mind, it is not a lot of sleep time. Less than house
watching TV, Netflix programs until 2:00 AM. After that I
got up and used the bathroom, then Ana got up and
used the bathroom. Systematically my world turned
back into the security world, way I laid there once again;
and receive my non-sleep award. I would lay there in
the bed sometimes thinking that I was dead; long
become my friend said the words Johnnie get up move
out again. I find myself back in Vietnam, that place each
night I see. For some strange reason, is always a part of
me, laying there with that thousand-mile stare. I know
how the hell, I ended up there. Suicide prevention stop
it now. First you had to find a way, but you got to put
both feet back on the ground. Laying in my bed last
night, I once again was mad; I hope you understand
what I have to say. Don't take it the wrong way, but the
stop suicide; understand how people think on that day.
Lying in bed on this day, I was talking to my father in
heaven: as I do each day and night. And I was mad as
hell and deep inside in my mind with the compensation;
speaking to myself I was crying deep inside of my mind.
And then I apologize my heart and my soul, because I
was a person that just could not handle it. I was in that

moment once again, of wondering why I cannot be blessed with his words and his presence; it was I who forgot that he was always there. Suicide stop it now! This is going on in my bed, while my wife Ana is asleep right next to me and has no idea what was going on in my head. This is not the medication nor is it the psychiatry, nor is it the therapy, nor is it the sociology, nor is it just the mythology many may think of. This is my father in heaven and I Johnnie H Williams Junior. There is nothing human for you to try to understand, it is our father in heaven, who allows us to walk the land. Each day that we live what the right or wrong, he shall decide which day and how long. I became so angry because I try so hard, to find a better way of life for all. Sometimes I don't understand that I can have my way; just because I love the words. Help is on the way! Today was one of the days, I turned out to be mad as hell. Laying there in your own bed, can this be possible? Deep in the world I live and in the world of many like me. This is the world of hell and I suggest you use my words. All of you would like to make a fool of me, there's no way in hell; don't ever ring this bell. Post-traumatic stress disorder. Stop suicide now. Which day would you like for me to start on? Which life which like me to start on, normal, fragile, diabetic, medicated, institutionalizing and let's not forget about 6B. Which is locked down for many

as me, who come home that really need it. for you who
are reading what I am writing, don't you ever take my
words on a joke. You are not there with us; you will not
want to be there with us; we would not want you to be
there with us. How many days of the week would you
throw up, how many days of the week would you grow
up. You know what it's like to come home alone! Do you
know how it feels on the battlefield when a woman or
man veteran dies? Were you ever there when there was
no more time for fear, because the only thing that was
there was death in the air? How many rounds that you
shoot, that your balls felt so loose. You thought it would
be over, until the next day, your back in the mud with all
the damned blood. High up in that chopper where they
dropped your ass off, the only thing you never thought
about; is making it back home. You to would think if you
would there, God bless America symbol; you know why I
care. I was angry as hell and I apologize to God is a
reason for everything. The reason we may not know! I
am not blaming my problems on anyone this you must
understand; I am the one who must walk the land. Do
not criticize yourself, for what you have been through;
get up off your ass and do as I do. If you are angry go to
the gym, go for that swim. Walk and walk and walk a
little at a time. Because summertime is coming, and
soon it will be hot and warm outside. Understand the
anger that we have inside, our father in heaven is
keeping his eye on you all the time. If you read any my

books you understand; our father in heaven is the one in charge of this land. Therefore anger, frustration, stupid-ness, irregularities, short tempered nests and all the above must change. Four strokes, three heart attacks, from nine months pregnant down to several months pregnant. Down to 220 pounds and on my new diet. All my anger will now be in the gym as my words say. I'll be back there to kick some ass again, all who are angry and mad you must learn to enjoy your life. Look in front of you now, before there is nothing left for you to see. I still see those who criticize also those who can care less, and I know the things I would like to do. Of the person of high security; at the number one position in the line of defense. I must also remember; I am a soldier in my father's Army; and await his orders. Suicide stop it now. The last thing I ever worry about, is being attacked by any human being, or numbers of human beings. Johnnie H Williams Junior. My psychiatrist Dr. Julia Golior is a special person in my life, and I talk about her since; is important that you find someone just like her. I won't go through all the things that I have been through, because it doesn't talk of all the things that you have been through. What I am talking about is all the things that we have been through, not the things that a person named me have been through. This book is about everyone who has had a problem in their life, every book I have ever written; I've used myself as an example. I'm the only person at fault and the only person to blame. There is no better writing about anyone, only how to live a better life; by walking out of that dark hold of darkness in my books I've written that I've been to hell, 10 times already and the devil was absent. As a scorpion and a Vietnam veteran I can understand why. My father in heaven had pushed many people on my path and this is because of the help that was needed. My psychiatrist Dr. Julia Golior of the James J peters VA Medical Center Bronx New York 130 West Kingsbridge Rd. is one of the reasons why I am still here today. Going through hell I was at a point that I was doing things and Dr. Julia Golior said I need to be locked down. I cannot believe this or that she had even recommended this. Here I was a man falling in love, going out of my mind, my trigger was cabdrivers. About the whip every cabdriver's ass In New York City! Besides hanging out in every bar in New York City and tried to find somebody to find to have a fight with. We had talked for several months and as a guardian angel; I could not believe how I was attracted to her words of understanding. For the first time in my life, there was someone that I was listening to beside Mr. Sampson.

There was something about her wording/understanding/chargeability/leadership/coordination. I loved it the way that she acted but is not like a follower which I hate but was like a leader in which I love. When my psychiatrist that I Johnnie H Williams Junior probably say who is still to this day. Dr. Julia Golior took me up to room 6 B lock down, I cannot believe that this was happening. My trust was all given to her and more ways that you may ever think, I have never had time coming home from Vietnam; ever given my trust to anyone other than Mr. Sampson. Don't even think about it! The James J peters VA Medical Center has been to change my life in many ways with all the people that are fully supportive of our veterans today. The problem with me being locked down, would you believe it this was a 21-day program. I did tell you I was a bad fell in Vietnam that I'm not, it goes to show you that a lot of people know that you have a lot of bad problems. It was in my 21-day program that I was supposed to be locked down, and other ways you can get out for the 21 days for any reason at all. Do you think it was my Vietnam nickname, the lawnmower? I don't know what happened, but we found out that 33% of veterans cannot be locked down overnight! I believe it was in my third day there Dr. Julia Golior came in and informed me that I was one of the 33%. I also believe one of the reasons was because, I walked around every night veterans were nervous; the arguments the farces the fight I just looked at them. somewhere along the way, I believe somebody said to not let this guy sleep here at night, you get the picture family. From that day I was there at 8 o'clock every morning and had to leave 3 o'clock every evening. This is how I did the rest of my 21 day stay and this is my locked down. I have the best psychiatrists on the planet, who have saved my life you must do the same. Find a person whom you can talk to, which understand you, but the real problems in your life. I'm hoping that you are understanding, life doesn't start just for you. I'm hoping that you are understanding. Life doesn't start just for me. I'm hoping you are understanding life is giving by our father in heaven and the hell that we go through it because we may never understand! Understand this there is a reason for everything, one of the reasons is why I am writing this damn book. If you the reader knows why you are reading this book. If you the reader knows why you are reading this book again. Did you not answer the question, of why you're reading this book; of the reason for everything and reverse psychology of the other systems of life and death and be on. Suicide stop it now there is only one way to do this and this is by reaching far beyond the mind can think, four different times of Russian roulette; 20+ time jump roof on the roof plus Exeter things and extremely stupid of the things that one could never think of. Outcome still alive for whatever reason that most wouldn't even think of,

42

waking up what morning where when how what mountain the side stream unknown. Can't remember how you even got there or what state. In your own apartment did not even want to make it. I think I'll stop right their suicide stop it now.

Are You Thinking About Yourself Again?

I want you to know it wasn't until I began, to study in psychology; that my brains splatter all over the place as I walk each day in that life. Unknown to many people there are many as me have this problem. Emile Durkheim was once a such person, who change my life. It was his study of the book called suicide that open my mind. I never read a book like this in my entire life and doubt that I will ever find one as powerful as it is. Nor do I think or understand many will comprehend the capability of going from the first to the ending page but the possibility of coming out as I have 100% understanding of what was said. Anyone in the need of help to stop what is called suicide thoughts must read this book, case closed. Space through the many ways and times and shapes and miles of roads and trenches, in which I have traveled there was a comparison that blew me off the river rock. Understand this is not a joke not a bull not way of talking, as it comes out of my mouth; into thy brain of facts which did happen on my tour of finding my way out. Not willing to go back and talk about Vietnam, it was never an easy way out for any of us God bless my brothers and sisters; it never stopped for a moment that we were there. He saw someone one moment and the next he saw someone else one was a friend the other was a loss moving forward case close. Had to sit up somewhere up in the sky, many times it was a rooftop; we jump from one side to the other side. Sometimes I was slip but who the hell would give the dip if I slipped. I sometimes would wake up in the morning, with a lot of pain got up off my ass and had another drink again. Are you thinking about yourself again, who the hell gives dame? Now living by myself, working two jobs; because I hate to sleep waiting for someone to shoot me while I'm sleep. They may not even know it I think I wrecked the car on the 45 miles an hour a few up in the even without nonmotor in the trunk like a sandwich and landed between the two like a McDonald's hamburger with cheese to share. I can't believe I got up and walked away from the accident, no human being can ever survive that junk. What the hell is wrong why do I keep doing these things, they keep me saying there is a reason for everything. Do you want to know how many of the times, that I tried to do other things? Most of you would only say, we knew he lost his mind anyway. Standing on top of the roof then I am looking at all those wonderful lights it wasn't until I went downstairs and made the phone call that I heard the Angle say in my ears. He can help you and he is always near all you must do is open your ears. All these things started that night I did not know, I was already in one hell of a fight. I had lost my father and my sister and my brother. And many of my friends I have been through hell and back and was fighting toward the end the anger and bitterness that has surrounded me was there to show me that it wanted me. Are you thinking about yourself again? The stand up and stand tall that was the night that I received my phone call. Yes I was angry and yes I was mad my father in heaven said you have to go through in order to walked this land, no one said this is easy no one said it would be great remember one thing you have to keep your faith. Suicide is a serious unforgettable irreversible never understanding subconscious event that most people do not come out of. Each damn time I have intended in, the door was shut in my face. I have seen myself in so many places throughout time only so many people understand this, and the rest don't, another reason why case close. Suicide is the number one reason, many do not believe, what others are telling them; that is still alive and passing this information on to them today. You in the world of psychology and study for years, your friends in the world of sociologists will also have studied hard; let's not forget our therapists who willing to put us back together in every way. Subconsciously close your eyes for 30 seconds 15 seconds of the 30 picks in this century, you can smell the pain of suicide from some century. Opening your mind for the last 15 seconds, understand how many times; I've already tried and failed plus realized I was wrong. This book suicide stop it now, you will now understand the willingness to live. There is a reason for everything, everything is not for you or me to understand and this you must know. The only reason is because I am telling you so, you don't have to be a believer; these are not my words that I say. Is my father in heaven, who has sent me out for another day. Each day that I stand as a soldier in his name, that I thank my father in heaven for the work that I do in his name each day. You must learn to stand tall and get through those things many call hard times, never fear when you know he is near. It Is Not wrong, to show your tears. Suicide always raise its head when people do not believe, the feeling is that you have had one I have been through. Trying to prove to many who don't believe, nor does willing to take into consideration what may even be on your mind can be true. They now call it PTSD part two, if you make it that far from the battlefield to the grave feel is not far. There is a better way of working together and a better way of saving lives by listening closely to what one is saying with an open mind. The numbers are adding up by the hundreds of thousands, every day is getting worse. Are you looking to your right, or to your left? Is it your friend or your neighbor, your husband or your wife? Love/Honor/Respect for all what it is that I'm trying to say I have been given a chance, to meet a wonderful wife Ana C. Williams and Christina J. Williams my outstanding baby girl an outstanding one of four magnificent family members throughout the land. If I did not slowly come out from where I was, this is the world I would have missed. You cannot be apologetic for anything because it does not work that way. A survivor as a person who was uncovered from the got damn avalanche and is still in recovery. Although he may not see it, they still do not understand who the hell you are. Not the person they want you to be. Whoever that is dumpy stand in front of me. Just in case you may think that I make an excuse, I say to you one time don't make that mistake. I'm still a scorpion I still have my machine gun and there is nothing I would not due to kick your ass. Johnnie H Williams Jr. I have respect for everyone, and I have served my country. I do not ask for respect, as a Vietnam Combat Veteran TET 1968. The respect is there on the wall in Washington DC and with all who have served and every war to protect America. Suicide stop it now, if you think this is a game I'm wasting my time telling you of some of the things that, not just veterans but amongst the living of every life, Take A look around your home, see other family members; look at them you see them you see me. Suicide stop it now.

Support Of A Better Way Of Living!

When one has been through what is called, the trust factor. This human being believes in you, or they don't. From the private sessions, to group counseling; sitting at home thinking to myself. The outcome one can never believe, in a satisfying way. At that point in time something is on my mind, it is safe to say what is on my mind? There are a lot of things I would love to do, like all the rest of us with through in our minds! I have learned to stand tall in life, with support of my father in haven! my life's there is trust; to the point where I work with an open mind. This was not an easy task for me to do, it was I who had to step forward and I who had to learn to separate. Separate all who were there to harm me, and all the ways that will unfaithfully be; treated by others not uncommon way. Once I learned to use my world, reverse psychology which allowed me; to not let them know I was aware of what they were doing. I was able to live a better life, being more aware of those who didn't care and those who will not share. I learned by helping others to live a better life, is one of the best ways to sacrifice; and enjoy this life. For me to see the smile on your face, will help me reach my 120 years as in my other books. For you and I to have good times and smiles on our faces will become a blessing for all. When we finally come into a room, where we sit down and talk of the future to come. Family this is one of the best ways, to work like the number one. Yes, help is on the way is my motto. This I will always say, along with the words God bless America. Each day. What you must understand if you were living in hell. I told you before the devil was absent, I have only one leader my father in heaven; not someone who was absent in hell. You are the one who is reading this book and I know you will understand thee outcome. I am still able to walk the land, with the help of our father. Whatever your doubts, whatever it is that brings your tears; God is always near. When was the last time, that you looked up and said the words? Thank you, father, for this day and everything in it. I laugh with my father all the time and I cry with my father all the time. You think that everything is in your time, you are wrong. I have thought of so many things which I believe should be done in my time. True that I did see the future, but the future that I saw was not my future. Of course, I was a part of the future, still to come and the best part of the future; is every one of us. When you are giving your vision, and many of us do not see

understand or have the time to think about it; they
don't even plant that tree. Have faith in thyself for its
the things in which you can do. Each time they call you
a fool, act as if they are not even talking to you. We
must all learn to have respect for each other, as well as
respect for ourselves. How you speak to each other in
the workplace, not how they speak to you in the
workplace. Do not act as others act toward you in the
workplace. What I found out; is they only see when you
act out; not when the others act out. Place yourself
about the rest, by showing your respect that you have
for all. If you know me and have seen me, my respect is
my honor, and this is my life. There is no reason for a
human being, to disrespect me in any way shape or
form. When this event does happen, the consequences,
should be not on the person being disrespected. First
comes my kindness with a smile and a blessing to my
father in heaven you are walking away case close. In our
world today there are so many people in need of help,
of course I know I'm not the only one here. But I do
know the job for which he has given to me, and I love
the job I was sent to do. If you try to understand, what
supportive better way of life is all about. You are going
out and finding something to do, with your life. Suicide
stop it now has a 1000% chance of working. How would
I know this I'm too busy, trying to care for more people
in this world than I have time to think of doing that
again? Each time I think okay be mad angry/frustrated.

My phone rings that moment in time, of somebody or a
guest speaker at 3 to 5 colleges on any given day. If so,
many giving things that I must take care of my wife
Ana/Christina my baby girl, I call see how she's doing;
then I might get some sleep that night. First you have
Ana C. Williams around the house all night, cooking and
caring for me. Then you have Christina J Williams, she is
up in Albany University and will graduate in May my
baby girl. I had to keep going on with the things that I, in
life which are not easy. If I stop what do you think is
going to happen to them. I had to get my head my butt,
and that was not the easiest thing to do in the world.
This is a few years for me to get my head straight, don't
forget the number of people that went to hell with me.
That I have no idea in that day and age or time in life of
what I was even going through. Mr. Sampson told me
the family don't know nothing about what you are going
through. 25 years later he told me this I walked to the
earth for 25 years. The words I speak are true the hell I
live in are true, I know you are either living there or not
far from going there. Find help now. Help is on the way
each and every day in support of a better way of living.
Your expectations in life, make you a leader not a
follower! For once in your life, can you take the time to
call yourself a leader; for the work in which you have
done. For once in your life have you looked around to,
indent 1/10 of a second understood the statement
being said by you; was that of a leader. One could be

born as a leader and learn from a leader the knowledge of a leader. One can come out of hell and lead as a leader of rising from hell. Only the wisdom of the moment in which the human being specifically engages talk, can specify the event. Not the one who beliefs what was being said about that event. When I close my eyes and I am in that event. It is that time that we are both together, asking/running/hiding/jumping/screaming; you will understand and feel the pain in which we are going through. As a leader in which you are going down that same trail, that we are you will go home with the same pain; that we have gained without a doubt. Our expectations in life are to help others never to live in this world of pain and misery in which we have for many years. Why do we say to you as a leader you must stand tall, it is because you must come out of it all? Help is on the way is every day. Our James J. Peters. VA Medical Center. 130 West Kingsbridge Rd. is only one of many centers in which you can find help. You must take the time to go and asked for help for any family member who may be in the need of help one day at a time. Don't let them point the way, as they had done for me for so many years. I was always thinking that there are so many willing to help me, and they were not. There are many reasons why I was used, and never even saw it coming. Everyone is not a friend and this you may think so is true; but that type of thinking is left up to you

because many of you still think It's true. At one time I
was going to add a list of names, that word be helpful;
but the few that I've used are the best. All who maybe
in the need of help, hope you find some that are the
same; plus get the same greeting. I pray that the
doctors and nurses and dentists is all the same and that
you thank God each day. Remember when I told you!
cannot Keep say I love you as a game each day, to try to
prove to someone how much you love them; it just
doesn't work that way. I stopped doing this because, I
found out in my head; one day I will be laying there
dead though words will no longer be coming out of my
head. If all these years I'm saying I love you dear, and
there is no response ,no tears the future? Veterans and
many families are in the need of help, suicide stop it
now is only one beginning; this gate is now opened to
all who want to step in. Of you who may not respect the
words. I do solemnly swear that I will support and
defend the Constitution of the United States against all
enemies foreign and domestic so help me God. I for
one don't know how long I'm going to be here; we call it
one day at a time. I tried to enter so many names into
this book, then I changed my mind; due to the fact your
name is already in it. Each time I written a book and I
said you the reader that was your name. Suicide stop it
now; is about every time you have gotten mad and each
time you would just about to go off; that one 30%
before you even heated up to go off that you never

even felt to go off. How many say how the hell did I end up here and to this day can't think about it. Have you heard people say they devoted their lives, to serving their country? Veterans are special for them bravery and their dedication to our country. To our family members anytime you feel, a veteran needs help there is a hotline; you can call the veterans hotline and they will help you. You can go to Johnnie H Williams Jr. on our Internet and find updates 24 hours a day. I'm trying to keep my 501(c)(3) up to date is kind of hard but I keep trying to keep it running. Which is help is on the way for veterans 1024 CORP. hopefully everything will be okay and I can do better. God bless America and help is on the way! Johnnie H. Williams Jr. 199th Light INF.4/12 (TET 1968).

Something That Is Most Important!

It has been the last two weeks, that I have finished this book. There have been several events, that have not been helpful in any way shape or form. Suicide stop it now, is a book that I am hoping will help many; to get out of the frame of mind that I have been out for years. This book is not to make money or fortune of fame, this something on my mind I must tell you. I must convince you just how real, this bad endeavor is hurting our world. By you reading the words of someone, who has not anytime to live. Is the truth that hurts and will set you free from this pain inside of me. Each of you who walk each day, inside of you there is this pain; the problem is you know it won't go away. This is the pain that is here all day and all night, many times we lose that fight. You see me with my joyful smile but never know the pain inside. The days I scream and the days I yell; how many days have I been in hell. Even the devil is scared of me and that's why he always climbs the highest tree. When you see your friends, or family members walking and living in pain. Your love can help them, stand tall for another day. Six months ago, I was a very sexually active man, until they touched me once and they touched me twice with their hands. This was called a treatment, which many have had; the only thing I know I no longer felt like a man. I'm telling you this because many things happen in our lives, and for the last six months suicide was part of my life. As I'm talking to you at this moment, I feel it in my heart sometimes I wish that it would never start. A lot of reasons that you may feel as I to, how can it take my manhood away from me to. I would only tell you this to stop you from what you want to do, suicide stop it now; this book will bring you a new way of thinking. Of all the junk that I was told and the reason that they said because of me that it happened. This was all on, as God is my witness. I am the veteran who will stand up and fight for you. With three heart attacks, two strokes; cut open like a hamburger. Back in the gym working out for six months I could not get it up. Even if I hit it with a hammer, three or four times; let alone look at my beautiful wife I want to cry like a baby. I cannot do the blame game or listen to the BS that I was being told, of why this had happened to me. I am a human computer and the facts do not fit. I found myself once again thinking suicide, were in the hell did this come from. Family the reasoning comes forth in one second, look at your family member; cools trauma is leaking all over the place right in front of you. Do you know and understand how many veterans I talked to each day and night? Am I a psychiatrist? No, I am not. It's when you have been on the battlefield together, that's when you have the right to talk to each other together. Blood sweat and tears comes from people calling you – suicide mold. We talked to them about talking to the professionals that can help them so many ways and then they call back and say thank you for your help and will continue to help them. When I heard what happened to the young lady and to my friend who is a cook on TV. That's when I made a couple of calls and I also want to talk to the publisher, but it was closed today. I just wanted you to know, suicide happens you must ask for help. I was mad for what they did to me, this was something that should have never happened to me. What was I going to take it out on my wife, how was I supposed to perform at home? Everyone knows how I feel about my father in heaven. With his help I'm slowly coming back, and I would've never thought this would happen to me. If I didn't have to support of my wife Ana. The road would have been rough for me to travel. Everyone who's on this road to suicide and everyone who may think you know of someone who may be on this road to suicide. Kindly give them a copy of this book and or read it to them. I am a survivor and it is my father in heaven who has allowed me to write these books. Allowed me to use these words, and hope that you the reader will stop and take the time to understand that your life can become wonderful/ joyful/ and outstanding if you get through this with the help that is there in front of you. This I understand and all the good things in progress that we are now doing.

To show you the way of the future, you must be here to understand and enjoy it. We call it help is on the way for veterans 1024 CORP. We have got to learn to ask for help, I did not do this because who could I tell about a sexual problem I was having. You Have said it was my fault, because I had gained weight. When I know others that are hundred and 20 pounds more then I and still making love. Stay focused on your life and remember suicide is one hell of a large event going on everywhere. You can pick up a phone of going anywhere and say to someone I need help. There is a reason for everything, this is my fifth time in the world of suicide, and it is terrible. We veterans have a saying. Here today gone tomorrow. I don't know, I don't know. This is the job I have been given and I don't want anyone to take it from me. Help is on the way is my motto and I told you as much as I can say.

Suicide stop it now.

Johnnie H Williams Jr.

199th Light INF. 4/12 (TET 1968).